American Frontier #13

D0171609

BUFFALO BILL
AND THE PONY EXPRESS

A Historical Novel

by Debbie Dadey
Illustrations by Charlie Shaw
Cover illustration by Daniel O'Leary

DISNEP PRESS

NEW YORK

Look for these other books in the
American Frontier series:

Davy Crockett and the King of the River

Davy Crockett and the Creek Indians

Davy Crockett and the Pirates at Cave-in Rock

Davy Crockett at the Alamo

Johnny Appleseed and the Planting of the West

Davy Crockett and the Highwaymen

Sacajawea and the Journey to the Pacific

Calamity Jane at Fort Sanders

Annie Oakley in the Wild West Extravaganza!

Wild Bill Hickok and the Rebel Raiders

Tecumseh: One Nation for His People

Davy Crockett Meets Death Hug

Lawmen: Stories of Men Who Tamed the West

FIRST EDITION
1   3   5   7   9   10   8   6   4   2

Library of Congress Catalog Card Number: 94-70798
ISBN: 0-7868-4005-6/0-7868-5004-3 (lib. bdg.)

Consultant: Paul Fees, Curator, Buffalo Bill Historical Center
Cody, Wyoming

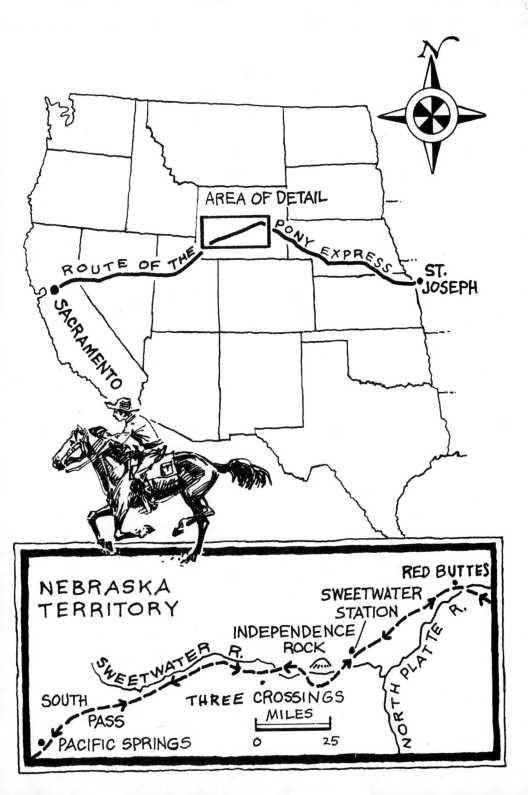

AREA OF DETAIL

ROUTE OF THE PONY EXPRESS

ST. JOSEPH

SACRAMENTO

NEBRASKA TERRITORY

RED BUTTES

SWEETWATER STATION

INDEPENDENCE ROCK

SWEETWATER R.

THREE CROSSINGS

NORTH PLATTE R.

SOUTH PASS

PACIFIC SPRINGS

MILES

0   25

The tall, thin boy pushed back the brim of his hat and read the flyer that was nailed to the door of the cabin. The wooden sign that hung over the door read: Central Overland, California, and Pikes Peak Express Company. Well, he thought as he knocked on the door, I'm mostly what they're looking for.

"Come in," someone roared. Inside the log cabin a man sat at a plankboard table cleaning a rifle. In a corner a huge bearded man sat chewing a mouthful of tobacco.

"Captain Slade?" the boy said hopefully to the man at the table.

PONY EXPRESS
Wanted
YOUNG SKINNY WIRY FELLOWS
not over eighteen. Must be expert
riders willing to risk death daily.
Orphans preferred.
Inquire with Captain Slade.

The man didn't bother looking up from his rifle. "Who wants to know?" he asked gruffly.

The boy took off his hat. "The name's Bill Cody, sir. I'm looking for a job with the Pony Express."

Slade gave the boy a quick glance, then resumed cleaning his rifle. "I don't need a stableboy."

Bill shook his head. "I'm not after a stableboy job. I'm here to ride."

The man in the corner laughed. Slade put down his rifle, looked at Bill, and shook his head. "Listen here, boy," he said. "We have mail to deliver over two thousand miles of the rottenest wilderness this side of Hades. It's a man's job. I can't use a little kid. Especially a skinny weed like you."

Bill stood five foot nine and weighed less than one hundred pounds.

"With all due respect," Bill said, "I was told I was too young to work on a wagon train, too. But I've been doing that since I was eleven. I've been riding since I could walk." He pulled himself up to his full height. "I can ride as well as any man, and better than most!"

"How old are you?" Slade asked dubiously.

Bill puffed out his chest. "Fourteen, sir."

The big bearded man in the corner snorted and spat an ugly stream of tobacco juice onto the dirt floor. "Heck, Slade," the man grumbled, "he ain't even out of his knee britches yet and he thinks he can walk in here and ride for the Pony!"

"Hold on there, Ed." Slade stood up slowly and gave Bill a long look. He rubbed his chin thoughtfully. It was 1860, and Slade had been the Pony Express division manager at Red Buttes in Nebraska Territory for about three months now. In that short time he had seen any number of riders come and go.

Riding for the Pony Express was tough and exhausting work. A rider was expected to average at least seventy-five miles a day, riding at full speed for six or seven hours. What made it even more difficult was that a rider on the trail was completely on his own and an easy target for whatever calamity might occur. The weather might turn so bitterly cold, for instance, that a rider could freeze to death; or it might be so hot he could die from exposure and exhaustion.

Riding so fast under such extreme conditions across all kinds of terrain, from mountains to deserts, a rider could be fatally injured in a fall from his horse. It was not that uncommon, either, for a rider to be attacked by Indians. Most Indians were peaceful, but often food was extremely scarce, and small, starving bands of Indians might raid an Express station searching for food. If they came across a lone Pony Express rider on the trail, they might try to steal his horse. Only one rider, however, had ever been killed by an Indian. The biggest danger for a Pony Express rider was horse thieves. Some of the gangs were ruthless killers who wouldn't bat an eye over shooting a Pony Express rider in the back. That was why the Pony Express preferred hiring orphans.

Slade blew out his cheeks and wearily shook his head. He didn't relish the idea of hiring someone as young as Bill. The simple fact, though, was that he needed riders, and this skinny kid was about all there was at the moment.

"Shoot, Slade," the bearded man complained. "This kid is so green he'll probably lame his horse in a gopher hole. Or he'll fall facedown in a river and drown!" the bearded man bellowed. Bill shot him a look.

"I swim as well as I ride," Bill said quickly.

Slade smiled at the boy's spunk. "All right," he said finally, "but I don't want to hear any bellyaching. I need a man for tomorrow's run." He pulled a pencil and paper off a shelf and pushed it across the table. "Sign the oath."

Bill eagerly picked up the paper and read:

While I am in the employ of the Pony Express Company, I agree not to use profane language, not to get drunk, not to gamble, not to treat animals cruelly, and not to do anything else that is incompatible with the conduct of a gentleman. And I agree, if I violate any of the above conditions, to accept my discharge without pay for my services.

Bill was proud to be able to write his full name, William Frederick Cody. When he was eleven years old his mother had been embarrassed that he couldn't write his name. As a child Bill had never cared much about learning to write. He preferred to be out hunting instead. But he hadn't wanted his mother to be ashamed of him, so he'd practiced writing his name everywhere, even on the sides of wagons and in the dirt until he could write it perfectly.

"Thank you, Captain Slade," Bill said after signing the oath.

Slade nodded, held up his rifle, and squinted down the barrel. "Ed," he said, "take this kid out and show him the ropes."

"Yes, sir," Ed said. He slowly rose from his wooden stool. He was a huge man, well over two hundred pounds, and he limped out the cabin door without giving Bill a second look. Bill followed him outside to a corral where seven horses leisurely grazed beside a barn.

Ed scowled at Bill. "It ain't right that a little squirt like you get a man's wages," he snarled. He spat tobacco juice into the dirt right beside Bill's scuffed boots. "Well, we'll just see how much of a man you are. Go on out there and get that black pony."

Bill swung his long legs over the split rail fence and walked across the dusty corral to the horse Ed had pointed out. The horse was shiny black with the Pony Express brand, XP, on her flank. "Nice piece of horseflesh," Bill whispered admiringly. He gave the pony a quick pat on the neck.

When Bill reached for her halter, however, the horse neighed nervously and suddenly reared, nearly kicking him in the face. Bill stumbled backward and tumbled hard onto the dirt.

Ed was doubled over and nearly choking with laughter. "What's the matter, baby boy?" he roared. "Is little Blackie too much for you?"

Bill jumped to his feet and squeezed his fists. "You should have warned me she was skittish," he shouted angrily. "I could have been killed!"

Ed shrugged. "If you can't take it," he said, "run on home to your mama, baby boy." He laughed again.

Though Bill was only fourteen years old, he had a man-size temper. And Ed's ribbing was more than Bill could take. He jumped back over the fence and swung his fist at Ed's face.

Ed easily dodged the blow and grabbed Bill roughly by the collar. "Listen here, you two-cent piece of tumbleweed," he hissed. "I'm going to tear you into fodder."

"What's the trouble?" Slade called out from the cabin door.

Ed dropped Bill's collar. "This little squirt was having trouble with a horse and tried to pick a fight."

"I thought you wanted to ride for the Pony Express," Slade said sharply to Bill.

"Yes, sir. I do," Bill answered. "But—"

"No buts, boy. I don't hire riders who can't handle horses. If you can't cut it, let me know now."

"I can do it," Bill told him.

"Then quit the fighting and do what Ed tells you to do." Slade went back inside the cabin and slammed the door.

Ed turned to Bill. His eyes had suddenly turned hard and mean. "Now," Ed told Bill, "go get that black pony."

Bill took a deep breath to calm himself down. For some reason, Bill realized, Ed had taken an instant dislike to him and wasn't going to help him.

"Fine," Bill said as agreeably as he could manage. He climbed back into the corral and walked up to the snorting horse. He began talking to her in a low, soft voice. "You're a good horse," he said. "What a pretty horse you are. You remind me of Prince, my first pony." He gently rubbed the pony's neck and ears. But the horse nervously pawed the ground and laid its ears back, a sign that something was wrong. Bill continued talking to her and petting her gently. After a while she settled down, and Bill noticed that she had straightened her ears. "Good girl," he said. Bill tugged firmly on the horse's halter and walked her over to Ed.

"Here she is," Bill said.

Ed scowled. "That don't mean nothing," he snorted. "Anybody can sweet-talk a fidgety horse. Let's just see how well you'll do out on the trail." Ed roughly slapped the horse on the rump and sent her back into the corral. He turned quickly and limped off toward the barn.

Inside the barn, Ed directed the boy's attention to the special lightweight saddles hanging on pegs along the far wall. "A Pony Express rider can't weigh no more than one hundred and twenty-five pounds," Ed explained. "If he's any heavier than that, he slows down the horse. These saddles are extra light to cut down on weight." He looked at Bill. "Riding for the Express ain't what you're used to, boy," he said condescendingly. "You'll find that out soon enough. After the first couple of miles your insides will be so shook up you won't know which end is up. But the Express isn't paying you to be comfortable."

Ed reached out and pulled down a saddlebag and tossed it to Bill.

"That's the mochila. The mail goes inside. Don't let nothing happen to it and you just might be all right. Lose it and you'll be out of here so fast your head will spin like a windmill."

Bill examined the mochila. It was nothing more than a thin strip of leather with padlocked pouches on either end. Ed called the pouches "cantinas." Besides carrying the mail, the cantinas also carried the rider's time card. The time card would be initialed at each station by the manager to keep a record of the ride.

There were roughly 190 relay stations along the two-thousand-mile Pony Express route that began in St. Joseph, Missouri, and terminated in Sacramento, California. Each station, also called a "swing" station, was about fifteen miles apart. They were called swing stations because that was where a rider would reach for his mochila and swing it onto a fresh horse. A rider typically completed the swing in less than a minute.

"Your route is from Red Buttes to Three Crossings," Ed mumbled around a mouthful of tobacco. "You'll switch horses five times." He pointed toward the corral. "Those horses out there cost the company about two hundred dollars each. So don't let anything happen to them, neither."

He took the mochila from Bill and replaced it on the peg on the wall. "You, on the other hand," he grumbled, "ain't worth a nickel. Remember that." Tobacco juice dribbled from the corners of his mouth, and he swiped at it with a dirty shirtsleeve.

"The trail won't be hard to miss," he said, "even for a squirt like you. For the most part it's the same trail used by the Overland stages. After you get to Three Crossings you'll meet the eastbound rider and ride back to complete the round-trip. You got it?"

"I understand," said Bill.

"Just make sure you don't mess up," Ed warned him. "If the mail doesn't get through faster and cheaper than our competitors', we can't stay in business. And if we go out of business, that means I don't get paid." His eyes narrowed to squinty black pinpoints. "If I don't get paid, I don't eat."

Not eating was the last thing it seemed Ed had to worry about, Bill thought, and it was all he could do to keep himself from bursting out laughing.

"Like I said already," Bill explained, "I understand."

"You're just a snot-nosed kid," Ed said, poking him in the shoulder. "You don't belong here. Come tomorrow morning you'll find that out and run on home to your mama. But for the time being I'm stuck with you." He tossed a brush to Bill. "Right now, make yourself useful by brushing down the stock."

Bill watched glumly as Ed turned and limped out of the barn toward the cabin. "Yes sir!" he said, giving Ed a sarcastic salute.

The fact is, Bill was grateful for the job—even if that meant having to put up with a snakebit sourpuss like Ed. Bill was lucky to get this job, and he knew it.

When Bill was only eight, his father, Isaac, had moved the family from Iowa to Valley Grove, a small farming community outside Leavenworth, Kansas. Not long after, in 1857, Isaac died. Though Bill's family was not poor, they had very little money. Almost everything they had was tied up in land. For a short time Bill's mother had tried to run a boardinghouse, but the Golden Rule House was never too successful. His mother was not strong and was often unable to work due to a variety of illnesses.

Being the oldest son, Bill was responsible for providing for the family, which in addition to his widowed mother included four sisters and a brother. Bill took any job he could find. For a time he drove an oxteam fifteen miles back and forth from a neighbor's farm to Leavenworth for fifty cents a day. He rode a mule as a messenger for the freighting firm of Russell & Majors and worked as a "boy extra" on their wagon trains.

In fact, it was while Bill was working for Russell & Majors that he heard about a new mail service the company was starting called the Pony Express. The Express was paying riders up to $150 a month, including board. That was all Bill needed to head straight for the nearest Express station.

His reception had been a disappointment. Instead of being treated as a man who was simply trying to provide for his family the best way he knew how, he was looked down as a silly fourteen-year-old boy.

"I'll show them," Bill promised himself as he brushed down the horses. "I'll show them all that there isn't anything Bill Cody can't do!"

CHAPTER 2

Bill was busy brushing down the ponies in the corral when he saw two men ride up the trail to the station. "Yee-haw!" Bill called out when he recognized one of the men. "Mister Hickok, good to see you again!"

James Hickok looked down from his big bay horse and smiled. "Well, if it isn't Buffalo Billy Cody. What brings you to Nebraska Territory?" Bill had first met Hickok a year ago while working as a boy extra on a wagon train. Hickok had given him the nickname Buffalo Billy after their wagon train had been caught in a buffalo stampede.

Bill stood up straight and bragged. "I'm riding for the Pony!"

"Well, how about that!" Hickok swung down from his horse. Hickok was clean-shaven except for a long, curly blond mustache. He was elegantly dressed in a tan duster, and around his waist he wore a bright red sash. The butt ends of a pair of Navy revolvers poked out from the sash. "I'm thinking of working stock for the Pony myself," Hickok said while gingerly rubbing his left arm. "I had a little scrape with a cinnamon bear and can't drive a stage for a while."

The man who had ridden in with Hickok got off his

mule. With his long shaggy beard and scraggly, mud-colored mustache, he was as sloppy as Hickok was elegant.

"Bill," Hickok said, "I'd like you to meet Moses Milner, better known as California Joe. He's a stock tender here at Red Buttes."

Bill shook hands with California Joe. "The wagon train drivers told me about you," Bill said. "You can shoot a flea off a mule's ear at five hundred yards and spot gold in a stream from a mile away."

Joe laughed and pulled his floppy hat off his head. "I've done a few things," he explained modestly, "but I'm not sure if I've ever done that!" Bill marveled that Joe managed to smoke his pipe, chew tobacco, and talk all at the same time.

"I'd say you're famous, just like Mister Hickok," Bill said, reaching out to take the reins from Hickok. "Let me take care of your mounts for you."

Joe slapped his floppy hat back on and shook his head. "There's no call for you to do that."

"I'd be proud to do it," Bill said. "Besides, Ed told me to brush all the horses. I don't want to miss any."

"Well," Joe said, handing Bill the reins to his mule, "I sure wouldn't want to deprive this here young feller the pleasure of brushing down this dirty flea-bitten mule of mine!"

Hickok laughed. "Billy," he said, "I reckon we'll see you at supper."

"You bet!" Bill said. "Nice to meet you, California Joe!"

Joe took his pipe out of his mouth and bowed before following Hickok into the cabin.

Bill led the mule and horse into the corral. For the remainder of the afternoon Bill kept himself busy brushing down all eight horses and Joe's mule. When he finished, their coats glistened. By the time the dinner bell rang, Bill's mouth was watering. "Some chicken and dumplings would taste mighty fine right about now," he said to himself as he hurried into the station.

Hickok, California Joe, and Slade were already seated at the table when Bill rushed in and sat down. "Sorry I'm late," he said. He looked over to California Joe. "I'm so hungry I think I could eat your mule!" he joked.

Joe leaned forward and whispered to Bill, "After one bite of Ed's cooking you may want to do just that."

They both grinned. Just then Ed came out of the small kitchen carrying a big bucket. He began spooning out stew onto each of their plates. "Much obliged," Bill said as Ed plopped a spoonful of food onto his plate. "I'm so hungry I could—" He looked down at his plate. He took his fork and pushed and probed around the plate. He stabbed at something that might have been a potato, and took a tentative bite. It was as hard as a rock. Bill put down his fork and looked forlornly at his food.

Bill thought back to the wonderful suppers his older sister Julia used to cook back home in Valley Grove.

"You going to stare at your food all night, boy?" snapped Ed.

"Is *that* what you call it?" Bill asked. Hickok and California Joe burst out laughing, but Ed suddenly went red with fury.

"What did you say, boy?" He thumped Bill on the back of his head with his metal spoon. Bill yelped and jumped out of his chair.

"Now hold on there, Ed," said Hickok. "The boy was only having some fun."

Ed had his lips pressed in a thin grim line. "Well, does it look like I'm laughing?" he asked angrily, staring hard at Hickok.

Hickok looked at Ed. "No, Ed," he concluded, pulling down on the ends of his mustache in an effort to smother a smile. "It sure don't." California Joe tittered lightly, then coughed when Ed turned and glared at him. It looked like Ed was going to thump him on the head, too.

Ed waved his spoon threateningly at Bill. "I don't take kindly to insults," he growled.

Bill sighed and shrugged. "I'm sorry for funning with you, Ed. I didn't mean nothing by it."

Ed muttered something that Bill couldn't understand, then turned and limped back into the kitchen.

Slade shook his head as Bill sat down. They ate the rest of the meal in silence.

When supper was over, Hickok sighed contentedly and pushed himself up from the table. "I reckon it's a nice evening to sit out on the porch," he suggested. Slade and California Joe agreed and got up.

Bill stood up, too.

"Hold on there, boy!" Ed was standing just outside the kitchen. "Get in here and do these dishes." Bill sighed and walked over to the tub where Ed had stacked at least a week's worth of dirty dishes. Ed tossed him a rag. "Make sure those dishes shine like brand-new silver dollars, you hear?"

"Yes, sir," Bill grumbled.

"And when you're done with that, sweep out the station."

As Bill began scrubbing, he wondered if tomorrow morning could ever come soon enough.

Bill could hear the men talking out on the porch.

"You reckon Majors and Russell can make a go of this thing?" Hickok asked.

"If they get the government contract they're after," California Joe said, "we'll all be sitting pretty."

Alexander Majors and William H. Russell were the two Missouri businessmen who owned and operated the Central Overland, California, and Pikes Peak Express Company. In April 1860 they founded the Pony Express Company, designed to be the quickest way for mail and small packages to travel from Missouri to California. Westbound railroad service terminated in Missouri, and until the creation of the Pony Express, mail had to continue on its way by boat or stagecoach.

The biggest competitor to the Pony Express was John Butterfield's Overland Mail Company, which had begun service in 1858. Butterfield stagecoaches took mail from St. Louis, Missouri, south through Texas, and then on to San Francisco. They ran semiweekly and covered the southern route in twenty-five days.

The U.S. government was one of Butterfield's best customers, and it was the hope of Majors and Russell that they could put Butterfield out of business and win the government contract for themselves.

"Well," said California Joe. "The country is getting bigger. Every day there are more and more folks heading to California. They'll be wanting mail service." He pointed the stem of his pipe at Hickok. "I ought to know. I was there in 1849."

"You and half the country," Hickok reminded him,

laughing. "Everybody was stampeding to get rich in the great California gold rush!"

Ed smiled, remembering his time in California as a prospector. Like so many of the thousands of people who thought they could get rich quick panning for gold, Ed had come up empty. A few lucky people struck it rich, but most folks went broke.

"Butterfield gets the mail through," Ed said irritably.

California Joe looked at Hickok. They both knew that Ed's temper was like a boiling pot. Once it got heated up, it didn't take much to get it to boil over. Ed was in a surly mood, and he was itching for a fight.

"True" said Hickok, nodding. "But by the time Butterfield takes the mail all the way down south through El Paso, Texas, and up again to California, the Pony has already delivered twice. The Pony's a straight shot across the country on fast horses in ten days. Butterfield's stagecoaches are too slow for mail."

Ed snorted. "Butterfield may be slow, but he doesn't have to cross the mountains in winter, or fight off Indians and outlaws. Those fancy folks in Washington are scared some important letter will be lost in the Rockies."

"The Pony hasn't lost a letter yet," Hickok pointed out matter-of-factly. "But you're right. If Majors and Russell don't get government help soon, I don't know how much longer they can keep the Pony running. It's costing them a fortune to stay in business."

California Joe relit his pipe and sent the smell of tobacco into the cabin. "When I was prospecting," he said, talking through a cloud of smoke, "we had a saying: Gold is where you find it; mail is when you get it. And we didn't get mail often. Why, I once got a two-year-old letter from Kentucky that came by way of the Butterfield route.

"Besides," Joe said, puffing on the pipe, "if war comes, the South will take over the Butterfield line. The Northern states will need the Pony Express."

For more than a year, states in the South had been threatening the federal government in Washington, D.C., to break away—to *secede*—to protect their right to own slaves. They were threatening to start their own government. There was even talk that the North and the South might go to war against each other. If that happened, the country would be split in half. Communication would be of vital importance to both sides.

At the mention of war, an expression came over Bill's face that was part anger and part grief. He was remembering his father. Isaac Cody had been an active member of the To-peka legislature at a time when the territory was being torn in two by those who wanted slavery in Kansas and by those who didn't.

One afternoon at Rively's Trading Post in Leavenworth, Bill had stood nearby as his father delivered a speech. Someone in the crowd had shouted, "Are you for slavery or not?"

Isaac paused for a moment, and the crowd grew quiet. Bill knew his father didn't believe in one man owning an-other, but he also believed in a state's right to choose for itself.

The crowd waited and grew restless. Finally Isaac spoke. "I believe in letting slavery remain as it now exists." A great roar of approval went up from many in the crowd. Others booed and hissed. Isaac raised his arms to quiet the crowd. "But I shall always oppose the further extension of slavery!"

There were more shouts and applause. Suddenly a man named Charles Dunn pushed through the crowd and lunged at Isaac with a knife.

Bill watched in horror as his father slumped to the ground. Then he helped carry him away from the angry mob. Isaac Cody never fully recovered from the stabbing, and attacks by proslavery ruffians against the Cody family continued for many years. When his father died, Bill blamed Dunn—and all proslavery ruffians—for his father's death.

Out on the porch, Ed sounded disgusted. "One thing's for certain. The Pony won't make it for sure if they keep hiring little squirts like that Bill."

Joe shook his head slowly from side to side. "Why don't you ease up on him, Ed," he said. "The boy's a hard worker."

"He's just trying to make a living like the rest of us," Hickok said.

Ed grunted. "All I'm saying is that this is no business for a little kid."

Then Slade spoke for the first time. "It's hard to keep good riders. Tomorrow's Thursday. If the kid isn't worth his keep, we'll find out soon enough."

CHAPTER **3**

Early the next morning Bill awoke suddenly to the sound of
yelling. He jumped out of his bunk and was just pulling
on his boots when Slade stormed into the cabin.

"Who brushed down the stock last night?" Slade
bellowed.

"I did," Bill answered.

Slade kicked a stool across the room. "I never want to
see a pitiful job like that again!" he roared. "Those horses are
our lives, boy! Now get your sorry backside out there and do
it right!"

Confused, Bill started to explain to Slade that he *had*
done it right. But the angry look on Slade's face told him
he'd better keep his mouth shut. Out in the barn, California
Joe and Hickok were feeding grain to the horses.

"Who taught you how to brush horses?" Joe snapped
when he saw Bill. He motioned angrily to the horses. Bill
bit his lip as he examined them. Their flanks were splattered
with mud, and their bellies were covered with burs.

"What happened?" Bill wondered out loud. "They were
perfect last night!"

Ed came limping into the barn. "Heck. I know what

happened," he said, pointing at Bill. "This here baby can't do the man's job he was paid to do!"

"You rotten bushwhacker," Bill snarled at Ed. "You did this!"

Hickok grabbed hold of Bill's arm. "There's no time for this," he said. "The stage will be here any minute. Let's get these horses ready." The Central Overland Stage used many of the same relay stations as the Pony Express. The stage would need at least four fresh horses when it pulled in for a short layover.

Seething with anger, Bill grabbed a brush and began rubbing down the horses. All he could think about was how much he wanted to take another swing at Ed.

Joe looked hard at Ed but didn't say a word. He clenched his pipe between his teeth and began whistling a tune as he helped Bill with the brushing.

Ed snorted, turned, and walked back toward the cabin.

"Don't you worry about Ed," Hickok told Bill as he, too, picked up a brush. "He's just rotten by nature."

"Anyway," said Joe. "It ain't Ed I'd be worrying about right now. If I were you, I'd be more concerned with my Pony Express route."

"What's wrong with this route?" Bill asked, happy at least not to be talking about Ed.

California Joe shook his head. "It's one hundred sixteen of the most dangerous miles on the Express," he told Bill. "You have to ford the half-mile-wide North Platte River, too. There's quicksand along there, and it's wicked after a storm."

Bill's horse shuddered when he pulled a burr out of its hair. "I can do it," Bill said softly. Then, in a louder voice, he said, "I have to do it."

"I reckon you mean that," California Joe said, smiling. "But for now . . . brush!"

By the time the stage pulled up, Joe, Bill, and Hickok had four shiny horses ready. Ed came out of the cabin and helped Joe hitch up the new team. Hickok tied his horse to the back of the stage and jumped up beside the driver. He waved to Bill. "I'm off to work stock at the Rock Creek station. Keep your eyes open out on the trail, Buffalo Billy."

"I will, and thanks!" Bill hollered as the stage pulled out.

Slade stepped in front of Bill. "You're up next, boy. The westbound rider is due in any minute. And for your sake, I hope you're better on the trail than you are with a brush."

"I can do it, sir," Bill said.

"Once you take that mochila, there's no turning back. The mail's got to go through."

"I understand," Bill said.

Ed walked up, leading Blackie by a halter.

"Got this baby horse all ready for our baby rider," Ed said in a taunting tone. He grinned as Bill took the reins.

Bill gritted his teeth. "Much obliged," he said. He checked the cinch on his saddle.

"Here comes the mail," California Joe hollered.

Bill looked up and saw the cloud of dust kicked up by the approaching horse. The westbound rider pulled to a stop and pitched the mochila to Bill. Slade signed the time card while Bill hurriedly adjusted the mochila and mounted the black pony.

"Good luck, kid," California Joe called out to him.

"Yeehaw!" Bill yelled. After all the trouble that morning, it was great to finally be on the trail. He hunched down into the saddle and let his body settle into the horse's up-and-down motion. "This is it!" Bill told himself. "I'm riding for the Pony!"

His horse flew over the trail. "You might be skittish," Bill told her, "but you sure know how to run." Bill pulled his faded red bandanna over his mouth as the wind and his pony's feet blew dust into his face.

As Ed predicted, the trail was not hard to follow. Since it was the same one used by the Central Overland stage, ruts were well worn in the ground from the ironbound wooden wheels of the stage. It was also the route used by folks in the thousands of Conestoga wagons headed westward to Oregon and California.

Bill quickly overtook the Overland stage. He waved at Hickok as he raced by. Stages could travel only about thirty-five miles in eight hours, and Bill knew he'd probably see them again on his way back.

Bill turned northwest alongside the North Platte River. In the distance he could see the ragged peaks of the Laramie Mountains. It was beautiful country, but Bill reminded himself to be alert for any movement. California Joe had warned him about everything from outlaws to snakes to prairie dogs.

"Prairie dogs ain't much themselves," he had said, "but one step in a hole while running at full speed can snap a pony's leg like a twig." A rider could be flung off the horse and probably break his neck. And even if the rider wasn't hurt when thrown, he could still wind up stranded miles and miles from a station in rugged country.

Before long Bill came to where the trail crossed the river. He carefully eased Blackie into the water. It hadn't rained lately, and the water wasn't very deep. But it *was* muddy.

"Dang!" Bill shouted as he was repeatedly splashed in the face. The river water reached up to his knees, and the splashing mud soaked his pants and shirt. To keep the mochila dry, Bill held the reins in one hand and the mochila in another. If Blackie got into quicksand, Bill remembered, he'd have to jump off and swim for it. Luckily they made it across without any trouble.

Bill gave Blackie a pat on the rump, slipped the mochila under him, and then slapped the reins. "Giddyap!" The trail turned away from the river. Blackie climbed over some shallow hills and then came out onto a long stretch of flat scrub. Bill had to smile. The early morning breeze was cool on his face, and he couldn't remember ever seeing a sky so blue. There was no one else in any direction for as far as Bill could see. It was just him and Blackie thundering across the big wilderness. "It sure is beautiful out here," he told Blackie.

By midmorning, however, the temperature had climbed to at least 100 degrees. Bill held tight onto the reins. The heat was making him sleepy. He pulled his hat down low to shade his face. Even so, the heat was unbearable. Bill had to keep wiping the sweat from his face. California Joe had told him about some riders who could sleep in the saddle, but he was afraid he'd fall off. He was tempted to stop and take a nap in the shade of one of the cottonwood trees along the trail. "What the heck," he told Blackie finally. "A few minutes' rest won't put us too much behind schedule."

Blackie was wet with sweat, too. Bill slowed her to a trot and almost stopped her. But then he recalled Ed's harsh words: "This baby boy can't do the man's job he was paid to do."

Bill shook his head reproachfully. "If I stop now," he told Blackie, "that would prove that Ed was right about me."

He gave Blackie an affectionate pat on the neck. "Sorry, girl," he said. "We'll have to rest later. Right now, we have mail to deliver."

It was then he noticed his horse's ears lying back flat. Bill looked around and didn't see anything out of the ordinary. But something wasn't right. He could feel it, and Blackie could, too. She wouldn't put her ears back unless something was wrong.

Just then three Paiutes on horseback burst onto the trail behind him. They were about one hundred yards back and riding hard. Their rifles were aimed at Bill. "Get going, Blackie!" Bill yelled. "I don't think they're going to invite us to a tea party." The pony galloped forward on the trail.

"Yeehaw!" Bill hollered as he hunched over Blackie. "We've got a race on our hands!" There was no way Bill could fight off three Paiutes with rifles. He'd have to outrun them. Back in Valley Grove, Bill had won most of the horse races he'd ever been in. But those had been for fun. This time the stakes were higher, Bill thought to himself. If I don't win this race, I'll be a goner.

Bill laid his body down flat onto Blackie's back, helping her run. "Come on, girl, come on!" The grain-fed horses of the Express were supposed to be fast and strong, Ed had told Bill. He hadn't said how fast, however. Bill hoped they were faster than the grass-fed horses the Paiutes were riding. Blackie's hooves pounded the ground, and Bill's heart pounded with them.

"Don't fail me now, Blackie!" Bill yelled as they rounded a curve at top speed. If we can just make it to the next station, he thought, everything will be fine. The Willow Springs station was close by now. More than likely, Bill fig-

ured, the Paiutes wouldn't bother getting into a fight with the men there, and he'd be safe.

Bill whooped. Up ahead he could see smoke from the Willow Springs station. "We made it, Blackie!"

Bill threw a quick backward glance down the trail. He was startled. "Why are they still coming?" he shouted.

As Bill rounded a clump of trees, the station came into view. "Oh no!" he cried out. The entire station had been burned to the ground.

There would be no relief horse and no help. Bill had no choice. He slapped the reins and kept on riding.

CHAPTER 4

BANG! A bullet went whizzing past Blackie's head. The Paiutes were close enough now that Bill could almost feel their eyes on his back. He ducked and held on tight.

"I wish I knew you better, girl," Bill said. Blackie was hot and tired. Bill wondered if she was the kind of horse that would just give up. She had already been pushed fifteen miles at top speed and now she was being asked to run another twelve.

"Come on, girl," Bill pleaded. "Faster. Faster!" Blackie responded to Bill's urging. Bill held his body close to hers and felt her muscles straining. When he came to the top of a low hill, Bill dared to look back.

"Yeehaw!" Bill hollered. "They gave up! Maybe they figured I wasn't worth the trouble." Just in case, Bill kept Blackie running at full speed and kept alert in case the Paiutes tried using a shortcut to head him off.

"Ed didn't know it," Bill told Blackie when he figured they were in the clear, "but when he saddled you up, he saved my life. I'll have to thank him personally."

Bill was happier than a tick on a fat hog when he saw the Horse Creek station up ahead. "Blackie," he said gratefully, "I could kiss you. And I think I will!" Bill leaned down to his galloping horse and kissed her sweating neck. He got a taste of wet hair, sweat, and salt. "Yuck! You might be able to outrun anything, but you taste worse than a bucket of sawdust!"

"Hurrah!" Henry Greene, the station manager, called out as Bill and Blackie raced into the relay station. "The missus and me heard about the Willow Springs station. We have the Willow Springs stationmaster and the hands inside. They got away just in time. We were afraid you were a goner."

"They couldn't catch me on Blackie," Bill said, grinning. He threw the mochila over the saddle on the relief pony and switched horses. "But I'm worried about the stage."

"They'll be all right. You just be careful out there." Greene stuffed Bill's time card back into the cantina and waved.

"Don't worry," Bill called out over his shoulder, "I'll keep my eyes open! Yeehaw!"

Fifteen miles of hard riding later, Bill took a quick drink from a bucket of well water at the Sweetwater station, threw his mochila over a fresh mount, and rode on. At Independence Rock, Bill had a notion to stop and carve his name into the granite. Rising 193 feet straight out of the prairie, Independence Rock had become an attraction for travelers headed west who would stop and scrawl their names into the rock face. But Bill didn't have time to add his name, so he just kept riding.

After changing horses again at the Split-Rock station, Bill followed a lazy mountain trail for a few hours and finally came to a rocky canyon called Three Crossings. It was named for a twisty mountain stream that had to be crossed three times. He gingerly guided his horse through the icy cold stream.

"I'd give just about anything to take a cold bath in that stream," Bill said. He'd been in the saddle for five hours, riding hard, and was worn down to nothing. When he saw the next station ahead he hollered, "Mail coming!" After so many hours in the saddle, Bill was relieved to finally stand up straight and toss the mochila to the waiting relief rider. In a flash the westbound horse and rider were galloping down the trail. The switch had happened so quickly Bill didn't even remember getting a good look at the rider's face.

Horace Moore, the Three Crossings station manager, laughed when he saw Bill walking stiffly to the well to gulp water from a bucket. "Don't drink the well dry," he hollered good-naturedly. "Better get a bite to eat. Sleep if you want. I'll let you know when the eastbound rider comes. It will probably be in about twenty minutes."

Bill dumped the rest of the bucket of water over his head. He was so tired and sore he thought he could sleep for a week, but he still had to ride back with the mail coming from the opposite direction. "Thanks," Bill said. "I'll try to push some of my bones back into place, too. I think some of them got bounced around a little."

Moore laughed again and started rubbing down the gray horse. Bill sat down in the shade of a tree and munched on a hunk of buffalo jerky. He'd only been dozing a few minutes when he was awakened by the call. "Mail coming!" He scrambled to his feet and ran to where Moore had his pony waiting. Bill swung up into the saddle but winced as his backside came down hard on the leather.

Moore snickered. "It's not exactly a feather pillow, is it?"

Bill laughed. "I've been on worse. Yeehaw!"

CHAPTER 5

Bill passed the Overland stage on the trail back to Red Buttes. From Hickok's call, "All's well along the road!" Bill knew they hadn't run into trouble. He was grateful to make it back to his home station without seeing any more Paiutes.

Bill was used to riding long distances as a hired hand on wagon trains, but he was not used to riding such long distances at top speed. His body ached more than a steer's hindquarters at branding time. After he tossed the mochila to the eastbound relief rider, he climbed down slowly from his roan pony.

"Well if it isn't our baby boy, little Billy Willy," Ed said as he came up and took hold of the horse. "Did that little ride wear you out?"

Bill immediately stood tall and tried not to show how tired and sore he was. He didn't bother answering Ed.

"Have any trouble?" Slade asked after signing the time card.

"Not much," Bill told him. "By the way," he said, turning to Ed, "thanks for giving me Blackie. She's a good horse." Bill smiled his biggest smile at Ed, then went to the well to get a huge drink of water.

"Take care of those horses," Slade said, nodding to the ponies in the corral. "And this time, do it right."

"Yes sir, Captain Slade," Bill said. After Bill brushed down the horses, he went inside the cabin and tumbled into his bunk and instantly fell asleep.

No sooner had he dozed off, however, than Bill was awakened by the noisy banging of pots in the kitchen. He knew Ed was fixing supper. The only thing worse than having his nap interrupted was the thought of having to choke down another of Ed's meals.

Ed was at the fireplace stirring a big pot of stew when Bill passed by on his way to the corral. "Thought you were going to sleep all day," Ed muttered. Bill sighed and hurried out the door. He found California Joe in the barn, his pipe dangling from his mouth. Joe was polishing a saddle. "All in one piece?" he asked as Bill walked up.

Bill gave Joe a weary smile. "It went all right, I guess. I had a little run-in with some Paiutes."

Joe started on another saddle. "Most Indians are peaceable enough if you leave them alone," he explained. "But when food is scarce it will get so a man would do anything to eat . . . even if it meant eating one of Ed's suppers!"

Bill grinned. "Also," Joe said, "I guess they don't like us tromping through their land. First the white man drove off all the buffalo so they couldn't hunt. Now we're driving *them* off by taking their land."

California Joe shrugged. "I don't know that I can rightly blame them for hating the white man."

"I reckon that's true," Bill said. He picked up a brush and began rubbing down a brown horse. He'd never had anything against Indians himself. His best friends when he'd been little had been two Kickapoo boys. He'd spent many hours hunting, swimming, and fishing with them in the woods near Leavenworth, Kansas.

"Anyway, it's not the Paiutes that's got me troubled," Bill said.

Joe put his brush down. "You talking about Ed?"

Bill nodded.

Joe sighed and shook his head. "Ed's been ornery ever since his leg was crushed in a buffalo stampede. Turned his wagon over right out there near the North Platte. Killed his wife and son outright. His son was just about your age, too. He's been mean as a hornet ever since."

Bill brushed for a minute before he spoke. "That still doesn't give him the right to treat me like dirt."

"Nope, it don't," Joe said as he checked the bay's hooves.

"I don't rightly know how much longer I can take his orneriness," Bill complained.

Joe studied the stem of his pipe. "That's up to you," he told Bill. "It seems to me, though, that fists aren't the best weapon in a fight with Ed."

"What do you mean?" Bill asked.

Joe tapped his forehead. "Use your wits. Prove to Ed that he's wrong about you."

Later, after cleaning up the supper dishes, Bill went out to the barn with a blanket. Joe came out and watched Bill make himself a bed out of the blanket and some hay.

"Figuring to watch the horses tonight?" Joe asked.

Bill nodded. "Slade's liable to kick me out of here if Ed messes the ponies up again. This way I can keep an eye on them."

Joe laughed. "Hickok was right," he said. "You've got grit."

CHAPTER 6

Over the next two months Bill's slim body got hardened by the riding. On his days off, Bill took Ed's orders and stayed away from him as much as possible. With each ride Bill made, however, Ed grew grouchier. Bill did his best to ignore him, but it wasn't easy.

Meanwhile, Bill and California Joe were becoming good friends. California Joe even agreed to teach Bill how to shoot while riding at a full gallop. "Let your knees tell the horse what to do, and that'll keep your hands free to shoot," Joe had told him.

Since he slept in the barn every night, Bill got to be good friends with the horses, too. Blackie was his favorite.

One day when Bill was brushing Blackie after a ride, Joe brought him a letter. "This just came for you from the west-bound rider."

Bill stared at the letter. It was from Leavenworth.

Dear Will,
    Mother is ill. Please come home.

It was signed by his older sister Julia. Bill stuffed the letter into his pocket.

"Is it your mama?" Joe asked.

Bill nodded.

"You'd better get home to her." Joe patted Bill on the back and left the barn.

Bill sighed and sat down on a stool. He thought of his mother. She had never been strong, and ever since his father had died she had grown weaker and more frail.

Blackie pushed her nose into Bill's hand. Bill smiled and patted the shiny nose. "I have to go, girl," he said. "But don't worry, I won't forget about you. I'll never forget the Pony Express."

Bill hated to leave his job. He went to Captain Slade and tried to explain. "I'm sorry to quit on you like this. But my father's dead and my mother's taken sick."

"You can go as soon as I get another rider," Slade said.

Ed stuffed a wad of tobacco into his mouth and leaned his stool back against the wall. "Just like I told you," he snickered. "You're a mama's boy."

Bill clenched his fists and looked at Ed with hatred. If Slade hadn't been sitting there, Bill thought, he would have laid into Ed like flies on a dead dog. But Slade *was* there, and Bill didn't want to ruin his chances of ever working for the Pony Express again. Bill walked out and slammed the door.

Three days later, Bill caught a freight wagon that was heading for Leavenworth. The wagon was empty, so during part of the two-week trip he stretched out on the wide dusty boards and slept. It was a bouncy ride, and occasionally the wagon hit a big bump. Bill would sit up for a minute, rub his head, then lie down and go back to sleep.

When they camped for the night, Bill stretched out on his bedroll and stared up at the stars. Most often his thoughts were of his mother. Would she be worse when he got home? he wondered. Would she be dead?

The wagon was thirty miles outside of Leavenworth when it started raining.

"Looks like a real gully washer," Bill told the driver, and pulled his wide-brimmed hat forward to keep the rain off his face. By the time the driver stopped the horses, Bill was soaked clear through to his skin.

"What's wrong?" Bill asked.

"I'm not going any farther until the rain lets up. I won't be able to climb out of the valley in this downpour."

I'm too close to home to stop now, Bill thought. He decided to walk the remaining ten miles to Valley Grove. Home was a log house set on the side of a hill. Bill didn't mind the walk, but by the time he saw his house he was not only drenched to the bone but also half covered with mud. The rain finally stopped when he was within shouting distance of the house.

"Mother! It's Will!" Julia cried from the door of their house. "At least, I think it's him," she muttered to herself. "I've never seen anyone so dirty."

But Turk knew. Bill's dog raced out of the yard and down the road. He jumped all around his master and barked. Bill knelt down in the road and hugged his dog's neck. "I missed you, too, Turk."

Bill's sisters, Julia, Eliza Alice, Nellie, and Mary Hannah, and his brother, Charlie, tumbled out of the house to greet him. "Phe-ew," Nellie squealed as she gave her brother a hug. "Will smells like last week's stew."

"Will, stinky!" five-year-old Charlie said, and held his nose.

Bill, who was always called Will by his family, laughed.

It felt good to be home. "That's a fine welcome for a home-sick brother!"

"You know we missed you, Will," Julia said. She took a step back and fanned her face with her hand. "But you need a bath."

Bill smiled, but turned serious. "First, I have to see Mother."

"She's doing much better," Julia said firmly. "And she wouldn't want to see you like this." She pushed Bill toward the well. "Eliza Alice, go get the washtub. Charlie, get the soap."

Charlie giggled. "Will's taking a bath and it's not even Saturday!"

After his bath and a change of clothes, Bill climbed up the creaking stairs and into his mother's bedroom. "Mother, how are you?" he whispered.

"Will! Come here, Son!" Bill walked to the bed, and his mother swept her arms around him. "It's so good to see you."

His mother's face looked almost as pale as the bedsheets, and she seemed even smaller to Bill than the last time he'd seen her. "Are you very sick?" he asked.

His mother touched her son's cheek and coughed. "I'm getting better each day. Julia was wrong to send for you."

"I'm glad she did," Bill said quickly. "I'm going to make sure you get well."

"That's my president," his mother said with a smile. When Bill was very young, a fortune-teller had predicted that he would grow up to be president.

Bill poured a pouchful of money onto the bed. "It's for you," Bill said proudly. "At the Pony Express I was making over a hundred a month!"

"Will, it's wonderful," his mother said. She brushed his hair back with her hand. "I'm so happy you're home, though. I was afraid you'd be bounced to pieces on one of those horses."

Bill smiled. "Don't worry about that," he said. "You just get well."

"I will," she said softly. "I will."

CHAPTER 7

At daybreak the next morning Bill was chopping wood and looking forward to a good home-cooked breakfast. After all the beef jerky and hasty meals he'd been forced to gulp down while riding for the Pony Express, his mouth watered at the thought of Julia's cooking.

By the time the breakfast bell rang, Bill had the woodpile stacked waist-high. "Smells good!" he said as he came bounding into the kitchen. "I could eat a horse!"

"Well," Julia said, laughing, "you'll have to make do with hotcakes instead."

Bill greedily dug into a plate piled high with homemade hotcakes, sourdough toast loaded with fresh butter, soft-boiled eggs, and bacon. He washed it all down with a cup of steaming hot coffee. "I sure would like some chicken and dumplings with custard pie for supper," Bill said as he helped himself to another stack of hotcakes.

"What?" Julia teased. "And here I was all ready to cook you a horse!"

"Julia, I pity the man you marry," Bill mumbled around a mouthful of food. "He'll be as fat as two prairie schooners from eating all your good cooking." Prairie schooners were huge horse-drawn covered wagons folks rode in when they headed west.

Julia stuck her tongue out at her brother, but Bill could tell she was pleased. It was hard to think of Julia getting married. After all, Bill thought, it wasn't that long ago that they were both children playing in the hayloft.

Julia called up to the second-floor bedrooms. "Charlie! Girls! Come and get your breakfast."

All at once there was a commotion like prairie thunder, and Eliza Alice, Nellie, Mary Hannah, and Charlie came clamoring down the stairs.

"Julia," Nellie cried, "Will's done gone and hid the baby dolls!"

Charlie nodded his head sadly. "The dollies are all gone."

Julia put her hands on her hips and frowned. "Will, are you teasing these children again?"

Bill shook his head and smiled. "Would I do a thing like that?" he protested innocently. "Wolves must have carried them off."

Mary Hannah stomped her foot. "Will, you give me back my dolly."

"Don't worry," Bill said. "Sit down and eat your breakfast. Then we'll go on a hunting expedition to find them."

"Hurrah!" yelled little Charlie. "We're going hunting."

Bill's sisters giggled and sat down to eat. Julia fixed a tray and carried it up to her mother's bedroom. But Charlie wasn't ready to eat. "Will, tell me about the buffalo and the cowboys. Tell me about the Indians and the Pony Express."

"Whoa there, just a minute," Bill said, laughing. He

enjoyed being with his family and loved telling them about his adventures. "One thing at a time. I'll tell you everything. But first, eat your breakfast."

Charlie sat down. "All right, but don't forget."

Bill promised, and Charlie dug into a pile of hotcakes.

Bill barely had time to finish his coffee before Charlie climbed out of his chair and tugged at his sleeve. "Tell me about the buffalo," Charlie said with his last bite of hotcakes still in his mouth.

"What about our hunting expedition?" Bill asked. "Don't you want to look for the dolls?"

Charlie jumped up and down. "First, tell me about the buffalo."

"Let's go up to Mother's room. Maybe she'd like to hear," Bill told Charlie.

"I want to hear, too!" his sisters all called together.

The entire family trooped up the stairs and gathered around their mother. Bill sat at the foot of the big wooden bed. His sisters sat on the floor on a big rag rug, and Charlie snuggled up next to his mother.

"You look a lot better today," Bill told his mother.

"With all this company, I feel like the queen of England," she said. "What's going on?"

"Will's going to tell us a story," Charlie said.

Bill's mother grinned and held up her hand. "Don't be telling us one of your whoppers now."

"Not me," said Bill. Then he winked.

"It was like this," Bill began, and suddenly everyone was quiet. "I heard the buffalo before I saw them. Next, I saw the dust made by their hooves. It was a mountain of dust headed right for me and my pony." Bill shook his head gravely. "A buffalo stampede is one of the worst things that can happen to an Express rider."

"What about Indians?" Charlie asked excitedly.

Bill nodded his head. "We're always on the lookout for Indians, too. Anyway," he said, resuming his story, "the buffalo were louder than a thousand charging ponies, and the earth shook and trembled! I thought it was going to open up and swallow my pony and me."

"Were you scared?" Nellie asked breathlessly.

"Naw," said Bill, shaking his head, "but my horse was. I've never seen anything like it. She just up and fainted. Luckily I jumped off her with the mail before she went belly up or I'd-a been a goner."

Suddenly Bill jumped up from the bed. "I tugged and pulled on that mangy bag of bones, but I couldn't get her up," Bill said, his voice getting louder. "And the buffalo were getting closer and closer."

Charlie looked ready to cry. "Will's going to get killed!" he wailed.

Julia laughed. "Charlie," she explained, "he didn't get killed. If he had, he wouldn't be sitting here lying to us now."

Bill ignored Julia and continued. "One old buffalo bull was heading right for me. He was bigger than our barn and had horns like full-grown trees. I did the only thing I could."

"What?" Charlie cried.

"Yes!" the girls echoed. "What? What?"

Bill paused dramatically, then smiled. "Why, I grabbed that old bull by the horns and jumped on his back. I had to get the mail through, you see, so I rode him all the way to the next Express station!" Bill nodded slowly, enjoying the children's awestruck attention. "I made it two hours early, too," he added matter-of-factly. "That old bull ran faster than any horse I've ever been on."

Julia pulled a face. "You didn't ride a buffalo," she said, laughing.

Bill looked innocent. "Sure I did." He smiled. "Why, there's not a critter alive that William Frederick Cody can't ride."

"Can you teach me to ride?" Charlie asked.

"Be glad to," Bill said, gently rubbing Charlie's head. "But I think we'd better start out with a pony and work our way up to buffalo."

"Then I can go with Will on his adventures," Charlie said proudly.

"Hold on now," his mother said gently. "I'm not sure if the world is quite ready for *two* tall-tale-telling Codys."

Everyone in the small bedroom laughed. Bill laughed hardest of all.

CHAPTER 8

I don't want you to go," Charlie whimpered. "I haven't learned to ride a buffalo yet."

Bill picked up his brother and hugged him tight. His whole family had gathered at the front gate to say farewell. Outside the gate was the dirt road that led back to Leavenworth.

"Don't worry," Bill told Charlie. "I'll be home again before you know it. Anyway, I have to go so I can get more stories to tell you."

Bill was sad when he said it. He knew it'd be months, or maybe years, before he'd get home again. But the family needed money. His mother had been feeling better for weeks, but Bill knew it would be quite some time yet before she could resume boardinghouse work full-time.

Julia tenderly touched Bill's shoulder. "Be careful out there," she said. Bill hugged her and then Nellie, Eliza Alice, and Mary Hannah. Then he turned to his mother.

"I'd hoped you could stay and go back to school," his mother told him.

Bill shrugged and smiled. "You know I was never much for book learning."

"Kiss me before you go," she said. There were tears in her eyes.

He kissed her on the cheek. "I'll miss you," Bill whispered. "I'll send money every month. Stay well."

Turk jumped beside Bill and barked.

"I wasn't going to forget you," Bill said, kneeling down. He gave Turk a quick, hard hug and stood up straight. He was thinking he might get teary eyed himself.

"So long!" he called as he started down the road. Turk raced beside him and yelped.

Bill shook his head. "Sorry, Turk. You stay here and watch over the family."

Slowly Turk slunk back home and Bill watched Julia close the gate. His family waved. He smiled, waved one last time, and walked away.

When he arrived in Leavenworth, Bill caught the Pikes Peak Overland Stage back to Red Buttes. The driver let him ride up top for free.

After bouncing around on top of a stage for ten days, Bill was more than grateful when the stage finally pulled into the Red Buttes station. He hollered his thanks to the driver and jumped down even before the stage had come to a stop.

Bill smiled when he saw Blackie. She was grazing in the corral and began neighing the minute she saw him. Bill walked over and rubbed her nose. "Hey, girl," he said gently. "It sure is good to see you!"

"Get your flea-bitten carcass back on that stage." Bill looked up and saw Ed charging at him across the corral. His limp was worse than usual.

Ed yanked Blackie's reins from Bill. "I told you more than a hundred times we don't need you around here," he said, snarling. "Why don't you go back to your mama?"

Bill sighed. Ed was as full of vinegar as ever.

"The hiring's not up to you," Bill reminded him calmly. "That's for Captain Slade to decide."

Ed spit tobacco juice into the dirt. "What I know is that we don't need another rider. We're full up. So get!"

Suddenly there was a familiar whoop and holler. "Mail coming!"

Ed pushed past Bill and led Blackie to the swing stop in front of the station. Bill looked down the road and watched as the rider appeared in a cloud of dust and slid to a stop. Slade signed the time card as the rider swung the mochila onto Blackie. Bill watched as the rider remounted, snapped the reins, and galloped away. In an instant the pounding of Blackie's hooves was a distant echo.

Slade turned, and Bill watched him walk back into the cabin. Slade's Colt revolver was slung over his hip. The captain didn't even bother to look at Bill; he just clomped up the steps, walked inside, and slammed the door shut.

Bill saw Ed grin. "Tough luck, baby boy," he called out as he led the other horse to the corral. "I *told* you we don't need you."

Bill cursed under his breath and angrily kicked a corral post. "You can't give up now," he told himself. He took a deep breath, walked to the cabin, and climbed the steps. He paused before knocking on the door, and sighed.

"This sure won't be easy," he muttered. Then he knocked, hard.

CHAPTER 9

alifornia Joe was watering the stage horses when Bill came back out of the relay cabin. "I heard you were back," Joe said. "How did it go?"

Bill shook his head. "No dice. Slade doesn't need or want me. I guess I came all this way for nothing. I'll have to find some other work."

"Don't get your bloomers all in a ruffle," Joe said with his pipe dangling from his mouth. "Things could still work out."

"No," Bill told him. "Slade wants me to leave on the next stage. Says he can't afford to feed any extra hands."

"The next stage isn't due in for three more days. A lot can happen before then."

Bill shrugged. "Well, I guess we can at least get some good hunting in."

"That's the spirit," Joe said. "I'll see if you forgot everything I taught you about riding and shooting."

Bill petted one of the horses. "Come on," he told Joe, "I'll help with the horses, and then we can get started."

For the next two days Bill tended to the horses and avoided Ed as much as possible. He spent all his free time hunting with Joe and even got in some shooting practice.

"It's a durn shame you can't stay," Joe said on the evening of the second night. They were in the barn, brushing the stock down before supper.

Bill plucked a burr off a brown pony. "It can't be helped. I don't think Slade's cared much for me since that time Ed got the horses muddy and blamed me. Besides," Bill said, laughing, trying to make himself feel better, "at least I won't have to eat Ed's rotten cooking anymore."

"That's true," Joe said, laughing along.

Bill heard the barn door slam. "What was that?"

"It's the wind, most likely," Joe said. He shook his head and stuck his pipe in his mouth. "Bill," he said, looking down at his boots, "I just want you to know that I've been proud to know you."

"Me?" Bill asked, surprised. "Why, I'm the one who's proud. After all, you're the famous one."

California Joe took the pipe out of his mouth and shrugged. He pointed his pipe at Bill. "You've got plenty of grit and determination, son. I know things haven't been easy since your father died and your mama took sick. But I don't think any man could have done better by his family than you." Joe sucked greedily on his pipe. "You should be mighty proud of what you've done, Billy," he said.

Bill blushed and looked away. California Joe put his hand on the boy's shoulder and gave it a playful shake.

"Besides," he added, "anyone who can put up with a grizzly bear like Ed has got to be pretty special."

Bill grinned. "Or pure loco!" he said.

The next morning Bill was cleaning out a stall when Slade tapped him on the shoulder. "You still want to ride for the Pony?" Slade asked.

Bill nodded quickly. "Sure I do!"

"Get ready. My rider's sick."

"I can do it, sir," Bill said.

Slade looked down at Bill. "Be out front in ten minutes. Ed has your horse ready."

Bill ran into the kitchen, grabbed some hard biscuits, and washed them down with some strong coffee. Ed came inside, and Bill could see he was in a foul temper. "Don't think this is going to make any difference whether or not you ride for the Pony for real," he growled.

Bill was too excited to spar with Ed. "I guess I'm just not that easy to get rid of," Bill told him.

"We'll just see about that," Ed said as Bill headed out the door and over toward the well for a drink of water.

Beyond the shade of the cabin, Bill was struck by the full weight of the morning heat. The sun was blinding bright and as brutal as a kick in the head. As happy as Bill was at the thought of riding again, he didn't look forward to ten hours of murderous heat in the saddle.

Bill took a long drink from the well. He had just poured a whole bucket of water over his head when he heard the call, "Mail coming!"

Bill dropped the bucket and ran to his horse. Slade was standing there, waiting to sign the time card.

The incoming rider tossed the mochila to Bill. Bill threw it onto the waiting horse and leaped on. "Yeehaw!" he hollered, and slid right to the ground with a thump.

Bill, the saddle, and the mochila were all sprawled at Slade's feet. "Get up!" Slade yelled. "Get this saddle on! Dang it, boy, can't you do anything right!"

Red faced, Bill jumped to his feet. He threw the saddle back on his horse. The horse nervously cantered from side to side, and Bill had trouble controlling her. Finally he grabbed the cinch. He was so nervous with Slade hovering over him, however, that he had trouble getting his fingers to work right.

Cursing, Slade roughly pushed Bill aside and tightened the saddle himself. "Any decent rider would check his cinch before he got into the saddle!" he roared. "What was I thinking hiring a kid?"

Bill flung the mochila onto the horse and climbed into the saddle.

"Try to stay on this time!" Ed snickered from the open cabin door. Bill shot him a dirty look.

"Get going!" Slade yelled.

Bill gave the reins a snap and galloped down the trail. Tears were welling in his eyes. All he had wanted was a second chance, and when he'd got it, he had messed it up. It's all over, Bill thought. Slade would never let him stay on as a rider now.

CHAPTER 10

Bill tried to forget everything and concentrate instead on
the rhythmic pounding of his horse's hooves. Still, he
couldn't forget. He knew that Ed had deliberately loos-
ened the cinch on his horse. It had been a mean and dirty
trick. And it had worked. Bill knew that all he could do
now was ride like the wind and try to make up for lost time.
He quickly switched horses at the rebuilt Willow Springs station, but Bill knew he hadn't made up much time.

He pushed his horse hard and made it to the Horse
Creek station not too far behind schedule. Back on the trail,
Bill swiped at his face with his shirtsleeve. The sun had
climbed high into the sky, and it was now hotter than a black-
smith's shop in July. Bill looked forward to a cool drink at
the Sweetwater station. But when he rode into the station, he
was surprised to discover that it had been abandoned. I guess
the company closed it down, Bill thought. Worse, Bill found
that the well had gone dry.

"Dang it all!" Bill said out loud. He would have to ride
the same weary horse all the way to the Split-Rock station.
"Sorry, girl," he said. He tapped the horse's flanks and
spurred her into a gallop down the trail.

Only two more stations to go, Bill thought. Then he

could rest a bit before he began his return run. Bill's mood had improved somewhat by the time he reached the Split-Rock station.

"Hey there, Billy boy!" The station manager, Hiram Plante, was a big burly man who always greeted Bill with some friendly words and a cool dipper of well water. "It's good to see you again. Where you been?"

Bill grinned and ran his bandanna over his face and head. "I ain't got the time to tell you now, Mr. Plante. Maybe some other time."

Hiram Plante shook his head. "How come you Pony Express riders are always in such a hurry?"

Bill groaned. It was one of his oldest jokes. Bill figured he must have heard it a million times already, but he laughed anyway.

Plante checked his pocket watch, then signed Bill's time card. "You're ahead of schedule, Billy."

Bill gulped down a second dipper of water and tossed it back to Plante. "It was nice seeing you again!" he hollered.

Plante waved as Bill rode out. "Take care, Billy!"

Fifteen miles later Bill galloped into the Three Crossings station. He had been in the saddle five hours and ached all over and was thirsty and hungry. There wasn't an inch of him that wasn't on fire from the baking he'd had in the sun.

Bill would have given anything for a dipper of water and a nap in the shade. He stood up in his stirrups. "Mail coming!" he hollered.

Bill could almost taste the stew the station manager's wife would dish up for him and could almost feel the cot where he'd catch a short nap before making the return route.

"I'll have a jug of water first!" Bill decided.

Bill was surprised that a relief rider wasn't waiting at the relay to take over. Horace Moore, the station manager, was standing out front with Bill's favorite horse, Blackie, but she wasn't even saddled.

"Where's the relief rider?" Bill asked. "Is he sick?"

"You could say that," Moore nodded. "He's dead. He got into a little misunderstanding in a poker game last night and got himself shot."

"That's too bad," Bill said, shaking his head. "Who's going to carry his route?"

"That's the thing," Moore said, scratching his head. "There isn't anybody to take his place."

Without hesitation, Bill piped up, "I'll do it."

Moore shook his head emphatically. "I can't let a boy like you take that mountain route. It's too dangerous. Besides, that's another seventy-two miles west through rough country, not counting the trip back."

"Just saddle up Blackie," Bill told him. "I can make it."

"All right," Moore said with reluctance. "Grab a bite to eat inside, and I'll get Blackie ready. You're going to need your strength to survive this ride."

Bill ran inside the cabin and gobbled down a plateful of Mrs. Moore's stew.

"Here, take these." Mrs. Moore pushed several hard biscuits and a few strips of bacon into Bill's shirt pocket. "I'll put some cold tea in your canteen. It'll keep you awake better than water."

Bill thanked her and hurried back outside. Moore was just putting the mochila on Blackie.

"Hello, Blackie," Bill said as he swung up into the saddle. "Looks like we're gonna have us another adventure." He was glad Blackie had worked her way to this station.

"Good luck, boy. You be careful out there!" Moore warned him.

"I will," Bill said as Moore slapped Blackie on the rump.

"Yeehaw, mail's coming!" Bill yelled. Moore shook his head as he watched Bill head west.

"You think he'll make it?" his wife asked him.

"I hope so," Moore said. "I hope so."

The trail was rough and unfamiliar, but Bill did his best to keep up his speed. Blackie's hooves pounded along the scrabbly mountain path, and Bill kept his eyes peeled for rocks or tree limbs that might be blocking the trail. Once he had to stop Blackie and walk her around a pine tree that had fallen across the path.

Bill laughed when he reached the next relay station. It was named Ice Springs because all year round ice could be found just a few inches belowground.

"I sure could have used some ice this morning when I was burning hot," he told himself.

When much of the trail was deep in snow, riding was more difficult and more stations needed to be open. But since it was summer, the Ice Springs station was closed down, so Bill just kept on riding. He was grateful, however, for the cooler, late afternoon air.

Bill leaned forward and patted Blackie's back. The trail had turned rugged, and Blackie was breathing hard as she scrambled up the steep, winding trails that snaked through the Rocky Mountains. Off the side of the trail was a sheer cliff. Occasionally Blackie's hooves would loosen some rocks. Bill would shudder as the rocks clattered and tumbled deep into the valley below. "I'm glad you're with me, Blackie. These mountains could be pretty scary without a good horse."

They were racing around the bend of a narrow mountain pass when Bill suddenly came upon a horse and man blocking the trail. Surprised, Blackie panicked and reared up, nearly throwing Bill backward onto the ground.

"Throw up your hands, boy!" the man shouted. He had a revolver drawn and pointed at Bill.

Bill pulled back on Blackie's reins. "I don't want to hurt you, boy," the man said, "but I do want that bag."

Bill considered reaching for his own gun but quickly thought better of it. He held up his hands and tried to look scared. If there was any way to do it, he planned to save the mail—and maybe his hide, too. A highwayman might have just killed an older man. "Looks like you've got the best of me," Bill said.

"Hand over the bag," the man demanded, still pointing his gun at Bill.

"Sure," Bill answered, reaching for the mochila. "I don't want any trouble."

"That's a smart little boy. What're they doing now? Hiring boys straight out of the cradle to deliver the mail?" The big man laughed and reached for the mochila.

Suddenly Bill squeezed Blackie with his knees, just as California Joe had taught him. Blackie lunged forward, knocking the highwayman backward. At the same time, Bill swung the mochila at him. The bag hit the man in the face, and he was slammed hard into the rock wall. The man's horse bolted and ran off.

Bill jumped off Blackie and drew his gun, ready to shoot. But the man didn't move from where he was slumped against the wall.

"Good work, Blackie," Bill hollered. "He's out cold. But I'm not taking any chances." Bill pulled the rope off his saddle and tied up the man's hands and feet.

"That ought to hold him until the station manager at Rocky Ridge can send someone out to get him. They'll want to lock him up before he tries to rob someone else."

"Meanwhile," Bill said after throwing the mochila back over his saddle, "we've got mail to deliver. Yeehaw!" Blackie and Bill raced off up the mountain path.

CHAPTER 11

Bill Reid, the Rocky Ridge station manager, took one confused look at Bill and asked, "Where's Charlie Smithers?"

"He lost a poker game and ended up getting shot," Bill said as he changed horses. "I'm taking his run tonight."

"He lost the poker game *and* got shot?" Mr. Reid shook his head. "Charlie never was very lucky."

"I left a little present for you on the side of the path about four miles back," Bill said. "A highwayman thought I was carrying money and tried to dry-gulch me. Blackie and I got the best of him, though. He'll have a big headache when he wakes up."

"More than likely your man is part of the Jack McCanles gang," Reid said. "He and his boys have been raiding Pony Express stations out near Rock Creek. Supposedly they steal horses, then sell them to horse traders down south."

Bill gave Reid a worried look. "Did you say Rock Creek?"

"That's right," Reid said. "Why?"

"Hickok's out in Rock Creek. You think there'll be trouble?"

Reid snorted. "Them McCanles fellers are meaner than a rustled-up hive of hornets."

Reid saw the concern on Bill's face. "Don't worry, son. If anyone can handle Jack McCanles, it's Bill Hickok."

Bill nodded. "I guess you're right."

It was dark as Bill galloped away from the Rocky Ridge station. From far off he heard the mournful howl of a single coyote. The only light on the trail came from the twinkling of the thousands of stars that filled the sky above him. Bill was dead tired, but the cool night air helped keep him awake. After riding this far, the last thing Bill wanted was to fall asleep and wind up tumbling off the side of a mountain.

"Wouldn't Ed love that!" Bill told Blackie.

The next station was Rock Creek. Bill immediately asked Horace Wellman, the station manager, about Hickok. Wellman said Hickok had gone out to hunt down some stolen horses.

"Was it Jack McCanles and his bunch?" Bill asked.

Wellman nodded his head. "You look sharp out there," he told Bill. "Those horse thieves could be anywhere."

Bill sighed. It would have been a lot easier riding off into the dark with a smile from his old friend. Bill took off on a fresh horse and tried every trick he knew to keep his eyes wide open. He even tried singing. But the mournful wailing of a coyote ended his concert.

"Well, Mr. Coyote," Bill said, sounding insulted, "the fact is that I'm not too fond of *your* singing, either."

It was just as well, Bill thought. "No sense attracting too much attention," he told himself. Night was hunting time for many animals, such as mountain lions, and Bill didn't want to be any critter's late-night snack.

After another hour of hard riding, Bill finally reached South Pass, which was not really a pass at all but a wide, slanted plain. It was also the Continental Divide, which marked the middle point of the United States.

Bill stood up in his stirrups and cheered, "Yippee!" The end of his westbound route wasn't much farther. Only two miles from South Pass was Pacific Springs, Bill's final westward relay station. Another rider would take the mail west from there, and Bill would carry the eastbound mail all the way back to Red Buttes.

It was ten o'clock when Bill galloped into the Pacific Springs station, right on schedule. He slowly got down from his horse. He'd been sitting in the saddle so long he could hardly straighten his legs. Now he knew why some old cowboys walked like their legs were curved arrows. After riding for so long one's legs bent to fit the horse's rounded body.

"Come in and get something to eat," Bill Whitlock, the stationkeeper told him. "The eastbound rider will be along any minute."

Bill followed Whitlock into the small log shanty and gratefully took a plate of stew. Whitlock kept shaking his head as he watched Bill gulp down his food. "Why don't you take a load off and sit down to eat?" Whitlock asked kindly.

Bill laughed. "Mister, I don't *ever* want to sit down again!" Whitlock looked puzzled, so Bill explained the whole story.

"I can't believe you're taking two routes," Whitlock said. "One is enough to kill an ordinary man, let alone a boy."

"I guess that means I'm no ordinary man," Bill said.

The stationkeeper smiled and handed him a cup of coffee. "Son, if you finish this double run, you'll be extraordinary. I've never known anybody who's done it."

Bill decided to take a quick nap. When the call, "Mail coming!" came, he jumped to his feet.

"Yeeahh!" he yelled. He'd never been so stiff. Instead of feeling refreshed, he felt as groggy as a bear in winter. He thought about the long return ride he would have to make back to Red Buttes and groaned.

Bill quickly swallowed a cup of coffee and hobbled out the door to the waiting horse. The coffee and night air revived him somewhat, and he jumped on the pony.

"Take care," Whitlock said.

"Don't worry, I will," Bill told him. "I've an extraordinary ride to make!

"Yeehaw!" Bill hollered into the night, and dashed off down the mountain trail.

CHAPTER 12

I'd like to lie down and sleep for a week," Bill muttered a
few hours later. The coffee had worn off ten miles ago,
but he wasn't about to stop. He had made it as far as his
regular route and was close to the Split-Rock station. It was
pitch black except for the stars, but he had no trouble finding
his way. He'd gone over this route so many times in the
months before his mother had gotten sick that he knew every
rock and tree on the trail.

At the Split-Rock station, Hiram Plante had cold water
waiting for him. It was so dark that Bill had to change horses
by lantern light. He tried to revive himself by splashing cold
water on his face. Then he was on his way again.

By the time he rode into Devil's Gate Gorge he was so
weary his eyes had begun to play tricks on him. He thought
he saw huge animals in the shadows that played on the canyon
walls. "Easy now," Bill told himself. "This is not the time
to go loco."

The hair stood up on the back of Bill's neck, and his
horse's ears lay flat when they heard a wolf's howl above the
roar of the water. "Maybe those shapes weren't my imagina-
tion after all," Bill said as he raced out of the gorge.

Independence Rock was an enormous black shadow

against the sky as Bill galloped past. The sun wasn't up yet, so Bill knew he was either on schedule or early. It was probably around four o'clock in the morning. By now his shoulders ached, his head hurt, and his face was chapped raw from the wind. He slapped his face to wake himself up. Only three more stations to go, he told himself, and then he could rest.

He was thinking about sleep when he saw the low flickering light of a campfire off to the side of the trail. A wagon train was camped beside the trail for the night. The white canvas of the Conestoga wagons glowed eerily in the darkness.

PING! A bullet zipped past Bill's shoulder. PING! Another bullet buzzed past his ear. "What in the world!" Bill yelled as he leaped off Blackie and fell to the ground, facedown. Whoever was shooting at him was a fair shot, and the next bullet might hit or even kill him.

"Are you crazy?" Bill yelled into the darkness. "I'm Pony Express!"

Bill waited. The shooting stopped. A man scrambled out from under his wagon and cautiously ran toward him. Bill could see his outline against the firelight and had his pistol drawn, just in case. He'd kill the man if he had to.

"Are you all right?" the man called to Bill in an excited whisper. He had an Eastern accent. "I'm sorry. I didn't know who you were."

Awakened by the shots, a group of men had quickly gathered outside the wagons. One of the men hollered, "John, have you lost your mind? You don't have to shoot at everything that moves!"

John shrugged sheepishly. "I thought he might have been an outlaw."

Bill scrambled to his feet. "Might have been an out-law!" Bill repeated angrily. He clenched his fists and stared hard at the man. Anybody as stupid as this greenhorn, he thought, deserved a good licking. "Mister, I'd surely love to bust your lip, but I've got mail to deliver." The fact is, Bill had to admit to himself, he was so tired that if he *had* taken a swing at John, he probably would have missed him and fallen down. So instead he pulled himself back onto his horse.

"Keep your trigger finger in your pocket," he warned the greenhorn, "and we'll all be a lot safer." And with that, Bill took off for the next station.

By now his horse was getting pretty tired. Bill frowned with worry. The Sweetwater station was abandoned, and he knew he would have to wait until the Horse Creek station to get a new horse. He sighed with relief when he pulled into Horse Creek. The station manager, Henry Greene, was out front; he didn't look happy.

"Sorry," he told Bill. "Darn thieves stole all our horses during the night. You'll have to go on with that one."

Bill felt his shoulders slump. "Was it the McCanles gang?" Bill asked.

Greene shrugged. "I couldn't say for sure."

Bill nodded. "I'll pass the word to Slade." He led his pony to the trough and let her drink. Then he remounted and rode off. He only hoped his horse could make it. She'd been running flat out for more than twenty-four miles. He'd never ridden a horse to death, and he didn't want to start now. If he was lucky, the thieves hadn't stolen the ponies at Willow Springs, too.

At the Willow Springs station, Bill whooped when he saw a fresh horse waiting out front for him. "Thanks, girl,"

Bill said to the exhausted pony as he switched mounts. "You did good. I would kiss you, but I remember how bad Blackie tasted."

In less than two minutes Bill was back on the trail, and rain began to fall. Bill was grateful that the ground was fairly level, because the pouring rain made it difficult to see the trail.

Bill hunched down low over his horse's neck as lightning flashed across the sky. He didn't want to make a tall target for the lightning. He felt his pony shudder every time thunder boomed overhead.

"It's all right," Bill said reassuringly. "You're doing great. There's nothing to be afraid of." When the rain finally stopped a while later, though, Bill figured he was just as happy as his horse.

Bill's eyes had gone puffy from lack of sleep. He twisted his hands in the reins for a tighter grip and laid his head on his horse's neck. Bill was glad when he finally caught sight of the North Platte River up ahead.

"Dang!" Bill shouted. The water was up by at least two feet, thanks to the rain. What had been muddy, almost stagnant water the day before was now a rushing, raging river. If he could just hang on, Bill figured, his horse would do most all the work of crossing the river.

Unfortunately, his pony balked when she hit the cold water. She reared up and neighed, refusing to go into the river. Bill held on and tried to calm her down.

"Come on, girl," he said soothingly. "I need you." Bill pleaded with the horse, coaxing her gently into the water. "I can't make it without you." But the mare refused and sidestepped the water.

Bill knew he had no choice. He jumped down, pulled

off his shirt, and tied it around the horse's eyes. "What a horse can't see won't scare her," Bill reminded himself. He pulled hard on her reins. "Come on, girl, I'll get you started." The mare stamped her hooves and snorted. Bill was so tired and weak he had trouble controlling her. He was afraid she'd balk and run back toward the last relay station.

But the blindfold worked. Suddenly the pony leaped into the water. Bill held on to the saddle horn and allowed himself to be dragged along in the swirling water. When the water was chest-high, Bill tried wrestling himself back into the saddle, but he was so tired that he lost his grip and slid off the horse. He came up choking and splashing in the freezing water. He lunged for the reins and managed to scramble back into the saddle.

"I haven't come this far to fail!" Bill told himself.

Then he saw the mochila floating away.

CHAPTER 13

Bill flung out his arm to catch the mochila, but it was just beyond his fingertips. "Dang!" Bill said, slapping at the water. The mochila bobbed just out of reach. He leaned out of the saddle, straining to grab hold of the mochila. Suddenly he lost his grip on the reins and slipped out of the saddle.

Bill tried swimming to his horse, but the current sucked him along. Too exhausted to swim, Bill closed his eyes and let the river pull him. He could feel himself sinking down and down. The roaring in his ears suddenly grew quiet as he was pulled under the raging white water.

Bill opened his eyes. He was underwater! All around him it was dark and as cold as ice. I'm drowning! he thought. Desperately he clawed at the water, trying to crawl to the surface. If I give up now, Bill thought, it will mean Ed was right all along!

Bill lunged upward and broke free to the surface. His lungs ached, and he coughed up water. But it felt good to breathe. His arms felt as heavy as thick pine logs, but he managed to swim. He nearly cried with relief when after an exhausting paddle his feet came down on something solid. He had made it!

Bill flopped down on the sandy bank of the river and rolled onto his back. He was wet inside and out. He was freezing cold, and he had lost the mochila. But he was alive!

After a brief rest, Bill stood up on wobbly legs. At the very least, he decided, he had to find the mochila. Even if he had to walk back to Red Buttes on foot, he was walking in with the mail.

After searching the bank, Bill let out a whoop of joy when he found the mochila snagged on some branches that hung out over the water. He plucked it off the branch, grateful that the mail was wrapped in oiled silk to keep it dry.

Now what? Bill thought. He had found the mochila, but what good did it do? He had no idea how far downriver he'd been swept. His horse and the trail were nowhere to be seen. He had lost his shirt in the river, and he was freezing.

Bill looked up into the sky. It was turning pink. The chill morning air had him shivering like a pair of castanets. But since he knew that the sun rises in the east, at least he knew which way to start walking.

The ground was rocky, and it was hard walking in his wet boots. In the faint early morning light Bill couldn't see any sign of a trail. Stumbling along, all Bill could think about was lying down and going to sleep.

"Don't stop!" he yelled to himself. "Keep going!" Then he stumbled and lurched sideways. His foot came down sideways on a rock. He slipped and fell facedown to the ground with a thud. Bill could taste blood in his mouth. His jaw ached and throbbed. Tears sprang into his eyes as he lay there with his face in the dirt.

Just then Bill felt the tingle of a wet nuzzle on the back of his neck. He turned over. It was his pony.

Bill was nearly delirious with joy. "Oh, girl, am I glad to see you!"

Blinking away his tears, Bill grabbed her reins and pulled himself up. He flung the mochila onto her back and then hoisted his right leg over. "Come on, girl, let's find the trail."

Bill laid his head on the pony's neck, and before long the heat of her body began to warm him. As the sun rose over the horizon, Bill found the trail and got the pony running on it. In front of him the sky was ablaze with yellow, red, and orange.

"C'mon, girl," he whispered hoarsely, patting the mare's neck. "We have mail to deliver."

When Red Buttes finally came into view, Bill sat up as straight as he could manage in the saddle. He knew he looked a pitiful sight. He was shirtless and covered with dirt. His jaw ached and was swollen like a melon from the fall he'd taken. But he'd made it! The tiny Red Buttes station cabin could have been a palace, he was so happy to see it.

"Mail coming!" Bill yelled. His voice was hoarse, and it hurt to swallow. Slade was standing out front with the relief rider, and he looked as angry as Bill had ever seen him. Bill was so exhausted from riding all day and night that he almost fell off the horse as he tossed the mochila to the next rider. When he got off the horse his legs buckled, and he had to catch himself by grabbing his horse's saddle horn.

"Where in thunder have you been?" Slade bellowed. "You were supposed to be back here yesterday! What have you been doing, fishing in the North Platte?"

Bill took a deep breath and steadied himself by holding on to the saddle horn. He looked at Slade through puffy, squinted eyes. "No sir," he said calmly. "I'm late on account of I rode a double route."

Slade turned his head sideways as if he hadn't heard correctly. "A double route?" he repeated. "What happened?"

"A rider named Charlie Smithers lost a poker game and got himself shot and killed. So I rode his route," Bill explained.

Slade scratched his head. "You mean to tell me you rode all the way to Pacific Springs and back?"

Bill nodded, then stifled a yawn.

"Why, that's over three hundred and twenty miles!" Slade said. "That's one heck of a ride."

An extraordinary ride, Bill thought to himself. He had changed horses twenty times, riding an average of fourteen miles an hour.

Slade checked his pocket watch. "That means you've been in the saddle nonstop for more than twenty-one hours!"

"Well, sir," Bill said modestly, "not exactly. I did stop just once to go for a swim in the North Platte River."

Slade looked confused, but Bill decided he was just too tired to explain.

"What's this I hear?" came a familiar voice from inside the cabin. "Buffalo Billy rode to Pacific Springs and back without a rest?"

Bill recognized Hickok's voice at once. Hickok strolled out of the cabin with a big smile on his face. "I always knew you were destined for big things. Fine job, son."

"Thanks, Mr. Hickok," Bill said. "I'm mighty tired, but the mail got through."

California Joe walked up and gave Bill a friendly pat on the back. "That's what we like to hear," Joe said. "Good work, Billy."

"You did a man-size job," Hickok said. "I guess we'll have to call you Buffalo *Bill* from now on!"

Just then Ed limped over. All Bill wanted to do was to collapse, but he wouldn't do it in front of Ed. Ed, however, didn't say a word. He just handed Bill a dipper of water, then led the brown pony into the corral.

Bill nodded his thanks and greedily gulped down the water. It tasted so good, he wouldn't have traded that drink for all the gold in California.

"By the way," Bill told Captain Slade, "all the stock at Horse Creek was stolen."

"That's why I'm here," Hickok said. "We're looking for some good men to help us round up those horses. We're going to rid this area of thieves for good."

"How about it, Bill?" Joe asked. "Are you interested in helping?"

"Sure," Bill said without hesitation. "But first, do you think I could rest a little?"

Hickok, California Joe, and Slade laughed. Then Hickok slapped Bill on the shoulder. Bill was so tired he almost fell down, but Hickok caught his arm. "You go ahead and rest. You deserve it. We'll leave in two days."

Bill lay down on his bunk inside the cabin and smiled. He had never been more tired in his whole life . . . or as happy. It had taken him twenty horses, more than twenty hours, and over 320 miles, but he'd finally proved he could do a man's job.

EPILOG

William Frederick Cody was a true living legend of the American West. In a lengthy career that included stints as a frontiersman, military scout, Pony Express rider, buffalo hunter, actor, and businessman, Cody is best remembered today as the owner and operator of Buffalo Bill's Wild West Extravaganza. This enormously popular Western theatrical featured authentic re-creations of life in the West and was a huge hit throughout the late nineteenth century with millions of fans in both the United States and Europe.

Born in 1846 in Scott County, Iowa, Bill moved with his family to Kansas when he was eight. When his father died, Bill became the main provider for the family. He rode a mule as messenger for a freighting firm, then worked on wagon trains heading west. Cody joined the Pony Express as a rider in 1860.

With the introduction of the telegraph in 1861, however, the Pony Express was made obsolete. Cody joined an antislavery organization and later enlisted as a Union scout in the Civil War. After the war he worked as a hotel operator and owned his own wagon train company. When both businesses failed, Cody was hired as a buffalo hunter by a railroad company to supply meat for its workers. It was his skill as a hunter that actually earned Cody the nickname Buffalo Bill.

After 1868, Cody scouted for the army in its wars against the plains Indians. In 1872, Cody tried his hand at acting and starred in many musical theatricals. He returned to the plains periodically to scout and to raise cattle. In 1883, Cody founded Buffalo Bill's Wild West Extravaganza. A huge success, the show made a number of tours throughout the United States and Europe. In addition to performances by Sitting Bull, the famous Sioux chief who defeated Lieutenant Colonel George Custer and his troops at the Battle of the Little Big Horn, the show featured the sharpshooting talents of Annie Oakley—Little Miss Sure Shot.

Cody performed with the theatrical until shortly before his death in 1917.

In fact, it was largely a result of Cody's Wild West theatricals that the Pony Express is today remembered as a brief but special time in America's history.